The All-Embracing Message Of Islam

Fi Rihab Al-Risalah

Sheikh Elnayyal Abu Groon

Outskirts Press, Inc.
Denver, Colorado

The All-Embracing Message Of Islam
Fi Rihab Al-Risalah
All Rights Reserved.
Copyright © 2009 Sheikh Elnayyal Abu Groon
V2.0

Outskirts Press, Inc.
http://www.outskirtspress.com

ISBN: 978-1-4327-3601-9

Library of Congress Control Number: 2009924050

PRINTED IN THE UNITED STATES OF AMERICA

About the Author

His Holiness Sheikh El Nayyal Abdel Gadir Abu Groon, a descendent of Prophet Muhammad (PBHH[1]), was born in 1948 in Abu Groon, a village established by, and named after, his renowned grandfather (H. H. Sheikh\ Muhammad Abu Groon) to be the home of his Sufi traditional institution. Unlike many traditional Sufis, H. H. Sheikh\ Muhammad Abu Groon (1860-1936) relied on unwavering adherence to *Taqwa* (God-consciousness) in endeavouring the deep realms of the Divine Truth, empowered exclusively by love of Prophet Muhammad (PBHH) and certainty about his path. His son H. H. Sheikh\ Abdel Gadir (1907-2000), the father of H.H. Sheikh El Nayyal, followed the way of his predecessor also through the love of Prophet Muhammad (PBHH). After actualisation of the Divine Love and the love of Prophet Muhammad (PBHH), he developed his own style of relaying the knowledge and wisdom of the Prophet (PBHH) and the beauty of following his path to attain good conduct, in a format of poems and rhymes, easy and perceivable by everybody. He raised his son H. H. Sheikh El Nayyal in this climate of the love of Prophet Muhammad (PBHH) and devoted him to learning the pure message of Islam in their traditional institution besides academic education.

Since his childhood, H. H. Sheikh El Nayyal followed the way of his forefathers in actualising Divine & Prophetic love. Moreover, he started exploring the sources of Islam: the *Holy Quran & Sunnah* (reports on Prophetic tradition) as well as the major works in Islamic

---

[1] Prayers and Blessings of God Almighty be upon Him and His family

i

thought and Sufism. His personal library includes thousands of books on the various sources of Islamic knowledge. He graduated from the Faculty of Law, University of Khartoum in 1970 and took a number of positions including being Judge in the High Court and Minister of Legal Affairs.

In the early 1970's the author wrote his first book: *Al-Sirat Al-Mustaqeem (The Straight Path)*, a comprehensive short account on Islamic theology. Many commentators at that time agreed on two points about this book: 1- It was the first rational and convincing argumentation of the core elements of the Religion, viz. *Islam* (surrendering one's self to God-Almighty), *Iman* (faith) and *Ihsan* (bettering one's worship) that tackles difficult issues like *Qadar* (Divine Decree); 2- Its style was unique in illustrating these subtle religious concepts as each and every word was very carefully chosen to serve the precise meaning intended by the author. Since then, and empowered by the love of Prophet Muhammad (PBHH), the author initiated a series of writings using his own unprecedented rigorous methodology of research. This included the following criteria for checking the authenticity of the *Matn* (text) of *Sunnah* and the accuracy of interpretations of the Holy Quran:

1. The authority of the Holy Quran and the protection of its text from loss and corruption are guaranteed by God Almighty: *"Indeed it is We who revealed the Revelation, and indeed it is We who are guarding it in safety"* [15:9]. Therefore, an alleged text of *Sunnah* or interpretation of the Holy Quran that conflicts its authority or protection, or contradicts its clear text should be rejected.

2. The Prophet Muhammad (PBHH) is the standard reference of Islam *"...and whatever the Messenger consigns unto you, take it, and from whatever he forbids you, abstain..."* [59:7] This entails that a believer should not disagree with him or disobey him, *"And We have not sent forth a Messenger but (for him) to be obeyed in accordance with the Will of God Almighty."* [4:64] Therefore, an alleged text of *Sunnah* or interpretation of a verse of the Holy Quran that supports objections or disobedience to the Prophet (PBHH) by any one

of his followers should be rejected.

3. The *Ismah* of the Prophet (PBHH) means that whatever he has said, done, or approved of was not just absolutely right but law, precedence and illustration of perfection, *"Verily, in the Messenger of God Almighty you have a good example (to follow).."* [33:21] Equally, his sanctity stems from his special relation to God Almighty, being the most beloved to Him of all His creation. This entails that his *Ismah* and sanctity should be preserved in all interpretations of the Holy Quran and narrations of the *Sunnah*. Therefore, interpretations or alleged narrations that violate his *Ismah* and sanctity, or contradict the aim of his Message, should be rejected and no weight should be given to the credibility of the narrators or to the authenticity of their sources. This means that the authenticity of the *Isnaad* (credibility of the narrators) does not entail authenticity of the *Matn (text)*.

In the late 1970's, the author launched a series of accounts in religious advice named *Al-Wasiyyah (The Kind Advice)* on theological conflicts, historical controversies, and contemporary issues in Islam. From the early nineties to 2006, elaborating on the same subject, he wrote a series of books named *Al-Rassa'il (The Messages)*, some of which resulted in hostile confrontations with the religious authorities in the Government of the Sudan. Recently, the author launched a series of books on *Revisions of Islamic Thought*, the first of which was published in Jordan in July 2008. The Arabic version of the current book is included in part one of this series and was published after being acknowledged by the Ministry of Guidance and Orientation in Sudan as a unique contribution to interfaith relations, tolerance, and coexistence.

Acknowledgement

I would like to thank Dr. Omnia Amin for initiating the translation of the Arabic version of this book. I am also grateful for Mr. Rick London for his editing remarks and for Ms. Diana Baker, Ms. Joanna Wilkinson, and Ms. Hilary Cumberland for their helpful comments. I also thank Dr. Abdalla Yassin OBE, Dr. Khalid Habbany, Dr. Manar Bushra, Dr. Mohammed Yassin, Mr. Mohammed El-Amin El-Tigany, and Dr. Saad El-Din Hussein for their contribution to the translation. Above all, I thank God Almighty for enabling me to attempt through this book to reflect a glimpse of Prophet Muhammad's Message and mercy to all humanity.

El-Nayyal Abdel Gadir Abu Groon
25 December 2008

Dedication

To all those who seek love, peace and happiness …

Table of Contents

In the name of Allah (God Almighty),
The Most Gracious, The Most Merciful

We have not sent you (O Muhammad) but as a universal Messenger to all people [34:28] [1]

O Prophet, verily, We have sent you as

1. an eternal paradigm, and
2. a bearer of good tidings and
3. a herald and
4. inviting (people) to God Almighty by His permission, and
5. a luminous source of light. [33:45-46]

---

[1] Note: The square brackets denote references to quotations from the Holy Quran. Due to variations in the translations of the verses of the Quran, the author did not restrict himself to a single source of translation.

Introduction

According to the *Qudsi Hadith[1]*, the mercy of God Almighty preceded His anger: **"Indeed, My mercy preceded My anger."[2]** This hadith may raise the following question: Were Messengers sent from God Almighty to deliver mercy to people or were they sent to set a scale of accountability to hunt down their mistakes for later punishment?

There can be no doubt that what the Messengers have delivered from God Almighty is mercy for humankind. However, a scale of accountability for people's deeds is needed to remind and show them where these deeds place them in relation to the bountiful mercy that their Creator intended and delivered to them. Knowing this, they are sure to abandon their errors. Hence, God Almighty overlooks their misdeeds and does not hold them accountable for the sins they have earned: *"Your Lord is the Most Forgiving, the Lord of Mercy, if He were to hold them for what they have earned (of sins), He would have hastened upon them the sufferance"* [18:58]. The Message of Islam is mercy from God Almighty if we agree that what had been delivered from Him through His Messengers is mercy for all people. However, some Muslim preachers chose the second part of the opening question as the main theme of their way of preaching Islam *(Da'wah)*. Thus, they used the scale of accountability to frighten, terrorize, and threaten people. They even drove them to a state of

---

[1] Qudsi Hadith is a saying of God Almighty, other than the Holy Quran, to Prophet Muhammad
[2] Sahih Al-Bukhari

despair and hopelessness from the mercy of God Almighty. As for those who do not respond to their terrifying admonitions, they are not only persecuted, but also executed! Therefore, they distanced people from God's mercy, while God said in the *Qudsi Hadith*: **"My mercy preceded My anger"**[1], as He also said in the Holy Quran: *"My mercy encompassed everything"* [7:156]. Isn't it more befitting for those preachers to present to the people this mercy which encompassed everything including anger?

The high moral qualities of Prophet Muhammad, may the Prayers and Blessings of God Almighty be upon Him and His family[2] (PBHH), are the embodiment of The Holy Quran, and he is, in essence, the mercy of God Almighty: *"And We have not sent you (O Muhammad) but as mercy for all the worlds."* [21:107]. In fact, Prophet Muhammad is inseparable from the Message he delivered, as God Almighty said *"... Surely, We have been sending Mercy from your Lord; it is He who is All-Hearing, All-Knowing."* [44:5-6]. Prophet Muhammad (PBHH) is surely a Messenger for all people, as God Almighty said: *"We have not sent you (O Muhammad) but as a universal Messenger to all people"* [34:28]. The Prophet (PBHH) also said about himself: **"Indeed, I am a bestowed mercy** (upon creation)"[3], thus confirming that he is the standard reference and that he is the mercy of God Almighty sent to all. Many people, however, committed the crime of separating the Message from the Messenger (PBHH), claiming the ability of interpreting the Message themselves, without the need to refer to the one who delivered it. Furthermore, they gave themselves the right to hold the Prophet accountable to their faulty scale of judgement in an attempt to find fault with his conveyance of the Message, as if God Almighty has not chosen for His Message the most befitting of all His creation in terms of knowledge, integrity of morals, and beauty of form! Little did they know that, consequent to this separation, they have grievously erred and strayed, through their misinterpretations and misconceptions, in

---

[1] Sahih Al-Bukhari
[2] Here, the Prophet's family refers to *Aal Al Bait* who are: The Imam **Ali ibn Aby Talib** – the Prophet's cousin and son-in-law - **Fatima AlZahra** – the Prophet's daughter and Ali's wife, **Al Hassan,** and **Al Hussein** – Ali and Fatima's sons.
[3] Al Mustadrak Ala Al Sahihayn

comprehending the mercy that God Almighty has bestowed upon people!

Prophet Muhammad (PBHH) also said **"Verily, I have been sent to perfect high moral qualities"**[1]. These are the moral qualities for which God Almighty had praised him and sent him to teach all people: *"And indeed, you are of a great integrity of morals"* [68:4]. Therefore, he was sent to complete and perfect the highest moral attributes, i.e.to approve and seal what has been preached by the previous Messengers (May the Prayers of God Almighty be Upon them) since they have all been sent to form virtuous communities. So, he is the seal of the Messages, the first in creation[2] and the aim *(Qiblah)* of the prayers (of God Almighty, His angels, and the believers). Since his Message is the all-embracing of all previous Messages, God Almighty made the Prophet's throwing His own throwing[3], obeying him is obeying God Almighty[4], pledging to him is pledging to God Almighty[5], and his order is the Divine Order of God Almighty[6]. He, thus, set him as the standard reference for humanity and the summit of the goal for those seeking human perfection.

---

[1] Musnad Ahmad
[2] **"A man asked the Prophet since when was he a Prophet; Prophet Muhammad replied: Before the creation of Adam."** – Musnad Ahmad.
[3] God Almighty says in the Holy Quran: *" ...and it was not you who threw (sand into their eyes, O Prophet), when you did throw it, but it was God Almighty who threw it"* [8:17].
[4] God Almighty says: *"Whoever obeys the Prophet has indeed obeyed God Almighty"* [4:80].
[5] God Almighty says: *"Behold, those who pledge their allegiance to you have indeed pledged their allegiance to God Almighty, the hand of God Almighty above their hands "* [48:10].
[6] God Almighty says: *"The command you make is not yours (but is in fact the Divine Order of God Almighty)"* [3:128].

The Aim of the Message

T he school of Muhammad (PBHH) is indeed the greatest school in the history of humanity, as God Almighty, in His Glory and Sanctity, has Himself praised its founder in His eternal speech for his high moral qualities and has sworn an oath on that. As God Almighty has the Supreme authoritative control over people, He is in no need to swear to them (by something) to reinforce His words or deeds! Therefore, His oath is but an assertion of the greatness of the one whom He has described and praised for his high moral qualities, and is not intended to make people believe Him. God Almighty says: *"(I swear by) "Noon"[1] and the Pen and what they write. By the Grace of your Lord you are not mad or possessed. And indeed you do bequeath rewards without boasting. And indeed, you are of a great integrity of morals."* [68:1-4] Therefore, Muhammad (PBHH) is the finest and greatest teacher in the school of human life, and for that reason he has been sent, as he said: **"as a teacher"**[2]. He was the first of all prophets to be created and the last of them to be sent with this sealing Message as the teacher for all humanity. God Almighty says: *"...and We have not sent you (O Muhammad) but as a universal Messenger to all people, a Bearer of glad tidings, and a Herald, but most people do not know."* [34:28] Indeed, this is the aim of his Message.

Prophet Muhammad (PBHH) has been sent as the divine example

---

[1] "Noon" is a letter of the Arabic alphabet
[2] Sunan Ibn Majah

of humanity in its perfection, to be followed by all people, imbuing them by his great morals and behaviour and leading them to the path of God Almighty without straying or faltering. People were drawn to him immediately upon seeing him and hearing him speak, as his manners were devoid of coarseness. God Almighty says: *"...had you (O Muhammad) been harsh or hard-hearted, they would have left you"* [3:159]. In him, souls found all they sought and loved. As a result, they became at peace and their anxieties disappeared as they perceived their purpose and their path was clarified by this great teacher: *"... and We have sent you the Revelation (O Muhammad) to clarify to people what has been sent to them"* [16:44].

This great teacher (PBHH) has been sent to the entire human race to teach them the high moral qualities which distinguished him from the rest of all creation including Prophets, Messengers, Martyrs, and Saints. The Creator of the universe, Supreme and Divine in His Domain, praised him for these moral qualities and described them as great: *"And indeed, you are of a great integrity of morals"* [68:4]. Prophet Muhammad the teacher of good conduct and humility said: **"Verily, I have been sent to perfect high moral qualities"**[1]. Therefore, even those who have faith and do righteous deeds are in need of him, for without him they are in darkness as God Almighty has sent him as: *"... a Luminous source of Light"* [33:46], *"...So that he may lead those who have faith and do good deeds from Darkness to Light"* [65:11]. This is the summit of the goal of what humanity can learn. He said: **"On the day of resurrection there is nothing that exceeds good conduct on the scale of a person of faith"**[2] and this, indeed, is the aim of the Message. Therefore, one should not think that devotion to fasting and night prayers is exclusively the worship and the aim of the Message, so that people may say that such a person "is the pigeon of the mosque" [3] (i.e. a devout worshipper). The people who fast and gossip slanderously about others behind their backs have actually broken their fast as if they were eating their flesh: *"... and do not spy, nor backbite one*

---

[1] Musnad Ahmad

[2] Sunan Tirmithi

[3] This is a phrase used to describe those who spend most of their time in the mosques

another. Would one of you like to eat the flesh of his dead brother? You would then abhor the one (who does that)!" [49:12] The Messenger also says: **"Many are the people who fast and gain nothing from their fasting except hunger and thirst"**[1]. Likewise, those whose prayers have not prevented them from evil and immoral deeds gain nothing from their prayers, since God Almighty has ordained prayer as a means of protecting its performer from evil and immoral deeds: *"Surely Prayer prevents from evil and immoral deeds"* [29:45]. Prophet Muhammad (PBHH) the most truthful of all speakers said: **"With high moral qualities a person of faith reaches the status of one who is devoutly praying and fasting"**[2].

As has been reiterated, high moral qualities are the aim of the Message and whoever is so described is, in fact, the closest to the Messenger of God Almighty on the day when one is most in need of salvation: **"Indeed, the most beloved and closest to me of you in the Hereafter, are those of the highest moral qualities."**[3]. **"It was said to the Messenger of God Almighty Muhammad (PBHH), that a woman prays the whole night and fasts the whole day but some of her words are harmful to her neighbours, he said: "There is no good in her, she is in hell."**[4].

Good conduct is distinguished from fasting and night prayer by lacking in boasting, conceit, and vanity that wipe out good deeds. It is also a virtue that extends to others in a manner similar to charitable spending. However, the latter might get affected by boasting and undue reminding of others of favours done, as the Almighty said: *"And don't remind others of favours (that you do), proudly boasting"* [74:6]. Therefore, the benefit of prayer and fasting does not extend further than their doer even if they are safe from afflictions, while good conduct is always safe from afflictions and moreover its benefit extends to others.

The teacher (PBHH) continued guiding people and clarifying the ethics and the high moral qualities to elevate them from the "darkness" of misconduct, rough dealings, tense relationships, and

---

[1] Sunan Tirmithi
[2] Majma' al-Zawa'id
[3] Sahih Ibn Habban
[4] Al Mustadrak Ala Al Sahihayn

3

expression of anger to the "light" of brotherhood, good conduct, love, and tolerance. He elaborated that: **"Religion is interaction with good conduct"**. This good conduct had been the foundation of interaction. This means coercion did not exist in religion in all aspects of life: in people's interaction between themselves, between a ruler and his people, or between people and their Creator, and even when preaching. The Holy Quran states: *"... Would you then compel people to become believers?"* [10:99]

Here the Message shines brightly to illuminate its aim clearly, as the Master of high moral qualities expounds: **"He who harms a *thimmi* (a Muslim follower of another Prophet) has indeed harmed me and will answer to me on the Day of Resurrection"**[1]. No one should be considered inferior or discriminated against because of their faith, nor should they be coerced to change their faith and forcibly accept another. It is a religious obligation for human beings to treat fellow human beings in accordance with their humanity, without compulsion or humiliation, as the great Teacher said: **"Religion is interaction with good conduct."**[2]

He exemplified this principle himself when he stood in respect as a funeral passed by. Then someone objected and pointed out that the funeral was for a Jew. In response, the Prophet (PBHH) said: **"Is he not a human being?"** When his companions once asked him to lay a curse upon their persecutors, he replied: **"I have not been sent to lay curses, but I have been sent as a mercy."**[3] A non-believer once entered the mosque of the Prophet (PBHH) and urinated in it. The Prophet's companions rushed to him, berating and terrifying him, and wanted to beat him up. The Prophet (PBHH) stopped them, consoled him and said to him: **"Arab brother, this Mosque is not intended for what you have done, but it is built for the reverence of God Almighty"**[4]. The integrity of the Prophet so captivated the non-believer, who there and then embraced Islam and prayed: "O God Almighty, have mercy on me and Muhammad but on no one else". The Prophet (PBHH) gently pointed out to him: **"You have**

---

[1] Kashf al-Khafa'
[2] Sahih Al-Bukhari
[3] Sahih Muslim
[4] Sahih Ibn Habban

constrained what is infinite"[1].

The Prophet had once been asleep with his sword cushioned underneath him, when a non-believer snatched it and said to him: "Who will save you from me Muhammad?" He said: "God Almighty". At that moment, the sword slipped from the man's hand and the Prophet took it and said to him: "Now, who will save you from me?" The non-believer said: "Your clemency O Muhammad". So, the Prophet (PBHH) there and then left him without compelling him to say: "There is no God but God Almighty" to become a Muslim. He said: **"He who kills a *thimmi*** (a Muslim follower of another Prophet) **will never smell the scent of Heaven even though its scent can be detected over the distance traversed in forty years"[2].**

---

[1] Sahih Ibn Habban
[2] Sahih Al-Bukhari

5

The Oneness
of the Message

All religions from God Almighty are Islam: *"To you (O Muhammad) we sent by the Divine Truth the Book, confirming the Books that came before it, and embracing them..."* [5:48], and He revealed each of them (Judaism, Christianity, and Islam) as a perfect entity with no defects therein. God Almighty said: *"... For All we have ordained among you a portal and a clear path (to God Almighty)..."* [5:48]. He also said to them (Jews, Christians, Muslims): *"...so pursue ambitiously the virtues and good deeds..."* [5:48] in order to create a virtuous community. However, people have distorted the meaning of the scriptures to serve their purposes. This act is unacceptable be it changing the meaning of the words or contexts, as it causes the apparent dissension and conflict between religions. This distortion, as disputable and unacceptable as it is, should still be dealt with in accordance with the aim of the Message, which is: high moral qualities, as they are the essence of interaction in religion. Therefore, the dissenter should not be coerced to give up what he believes in as it is up to God Almighty to judge his case, as He said: *"...to God Almighty you shall all return; and He will then inform you on what you used to dissent in"* [5:48]. As to those who remained unwaveringly committed to the original scriptures of their religion, they shall have their reward from God Almighty, Glory be to Him, who said: *"Surely, those who have faith (in that which is revealed unto you, O Muhammad)*, **and those who follow the Jewish scriptures, and the Christians and the Sabians, whosoever believes in God Almighty and the Day After** *(the Day of Judgement)*, **and does good deeds will have their reward from their Lord; and neither shall fear befall on them nor shall they grieve.**" [2:62].

The Book of the Jews comprises the *Commandments* and the *Torah* that God Almighty has revealed unto His Messenger Moses, may peace be upon him, and He named it the *Book of Moses* as God Almighty said: **"And before this, was the Book of Moses sent as a guide and mercy: and this Book** *(the Quran)* **which confirms it, sent in an Arabic tongue, is to forewarn the wrongdoers and to give glad tidings to those who better their conduct"** [46:12]. Therefore, since the *Torah* is a Holy Book, whoever denies it has surely rejected what has been revealed unto Prophet Muhammad (PBHH). Moreover, the Law of the Torah has been endorsed by God Almighty in the Message of Prophet Muhammad (PBHH) in his Book - the Holy Quran: *"We ordained therein (in the Torah) for them that: a life for a life, an eye for an eye, a nose for a nose, an ear for an ear, a tooth for a tooth, and for wounds their equivalent in seeking justice, and whoever grants his forgiveness, this shall be atonement for him. And those who do not judge by what God Almighty has revealed are indeed the wrongdoers."* [5:45] This surely proves that Islam is in fact the Message of God Almighty sent through all His Messengers to people from the time of Prophet Adam to Prophet Muhammad (Prayers and Blessings be Upon Them)[1].

The Holy Quran also reveals: *"And we followed in their footsteps (of those prophets) with Jesus the son of Mary, confirming the Torah that is before him, and We gave him the Injeel (The Gospel), wherein there is guidance and light, and confirming the Torah that is before it, and being a guidance and an exhortation to those who are heedful of God Almighty"* [5:46]. The Book of the Christians is the Gospel which God Almighty had revealed unto Jesus the Son of Mary and Spirit of God Almighty, may peace be upon him. It is a sacred book from God Almighty and whoever denies it has in fact denied faith in what has been sent to Prophet Muhammad (PBHH). The Gospel that has not been meddled

---

[1] All Messengers are equal in delivering the same Message of Islam

with is the divine truth. Today, Christians have all the right to adjudge by it and they are not to be asked to leave it and believe in something else, as some Muslims think. Some of these afore-mentioned Muslims overzealously call for the use of force to cause the people of the Book (the Christians & the Jews) to abandon their divine portal and their God-ordained path in order to follow them, while The Almighty says: *"So, the people of the Injeel (Gospel) should judge by what God Almighty has revealed therein."* [5:47]. If the Jews and Christians had explicitly conformed to their Holy Books without distorting them, they would have reached a state of transcendence which God Almighty describes as such: *"If they had effected the Torah and the Injeel (Bible) and that which was revealed unto them from their Lord, they would have certainly enjoyed abundance from above and from underfoot."* [5:66]. Despite their distortion of the Holy Books sent to them, The Almighty said: *"Among them are people committed to the divine path but the deeds of many of them are unrighteous"* [5:66]. Today, fault can only be found in their not bringing into effect the unadulterated teachings of the Torah and the *Injeel*; and not in their embracing of Judaism and Christianity! The Almighty said: *"Say (O Muhammad), 'O People of the Book! You are unto naught till you effect the Torah and the Injeel (Bible) and what had been revealed unto you from your Lord."* [5:68]. Jesus, the son of Mary, peace be upon him, came to endorse Moses, peace be upon him, and his Book. Also, the Gospel confirms Moses' Torah, further affirming the oneness of the Message, which is the all-embracing Islam. The Almighty said: *"Jesus, the son of Mary, said: "O children of Israel! I am the Messenger of God Almighty sent to you, confirming the Torah before me, and heralding the arrival of a Messenger coming after me, whose name is Ahmed (all-embracing for all blessings)."* [61:6]

The Book of the Muslims is the Holy Quran of Muhammad (PBHH) as revealed by God Almighty unto him: *"...confirming the Books that came before it, and embracing them"* [5:48]. In pertinence to this, God Almighty said: *"Indeed, the religion to God Almighty is Islam"* [3:19] meaning that all the religions delivered by the Messengers (peace be upon them) convey one Message which is: there is no God but God Almighty - and this is the all-embracing

Islam. *"Those who deny God Almighty and His Messengers, by segregating between God Almighty and His Messengers, and saying: "We believe in some and deny others", wanting to create a dividing path - truly, those are the disbelievers; and We have prepared for the disbelievers a humiliating sufferance."* [4:150-1]. Islam preserved the sanctity of the places of worship in all faiths without discriminating between them. The Almighty says: *"Had it not been for the intervention of God Almighty: safeguarding people by each other, there would surely have been destroyed monasteries, churches, synagogues, and mosques, in which the name of God Almighty is abundantly praised."* [22:40]. It is therefore all Muslims duty to respect all places of worship, be it a hermitage, church, synagogue or monastery. They should not depreciate any of these places, but should revere their sacredness as they respect the sacredness of the Mosque. Since: *"...those who follow the Jewish scriptures, and the Christians and the Sabians, whosoever believes in God Almighty and the Day After (the Day of Judgement), and does good deeds will have their reward from their Lord; and neither shall fear befall on them nor shall they grieve,"* [2:62] this means that their religion is Islam because God Almighty has accepted them as such – and He does not accept anything but Islam – as He said: *"and whosoever seeks a religion other than Islam (the all-embracing Islam), it will not be accepted from him"* [3:85]; and also because all Messengers have been sent with this one Message.

The Almighty said: *"Wherein God Almighty undertook the covenant of the Prophets: Regarding that which I have bestowed upon you of Books and Wisdom, heralded by the advent of a Messenger confirming that which you have, you are to believe in him and to champion him. He said: "Do you consent (to this Covenant) and pledge to be bound by it to Me?" They said: "We do consent." He said: "So bear witness, and I shall be with you among those who bear witness.""* [3:81] This asserts the all-embracing nature of the Message of Prophet Muhammad and the fact that none of the Messengers or Prophets has deviated from its path. It is from here that the oneness of the Message stems. Since God Almighty has undertaken a covenant from all His Prophets and Messengers (and consequently their followers) to believe in His Messenger, Muhammad (PBHH), this entails following his way and championing him in what he brought forth; and God Almighty made them attest to that and He, Glory be to Him, also bore witness with them! So, no Messenger has been sent without Prophet Muhammad (PBHH) having approved what he was sent to deliver. Therefore, it is a religious obligation to believe in all the Messengers and their Messages. None of them has deviated from Islam, which is the religion pertaining to God Almighty for which He has undertaken the covenant of the Prophets and Messengers, to accede to Prophet Muhammad (PBHH). Therefore, whoever repudiates anything in the preceding religions, has in fact denied their endorsement by the Prophet Muhammad (PBHH).

Worship *(I'badah)*

I f God Almighty requires His creation to worship Him according to His words: ***"And I have not created the jinn and the humans but to worship Me"*** [51:56], that is to say *"to know Me"*, then this implies that his worshippers should follow His Messengers to know what He requires from them by way of living in all aspects of life. As the Almighty said: ***"Surely, We have sent Our Messengers with Reasoning and Prodigies and with them we revealed the Book and the Scale of Justice, so people may conduct themselves with fairness"*** [57:25]. This is what God Almighty requires from people: *"...so people may conduct themselves with fairness"*, and to this aim He has sent all His Messengers. He endorsed them with the prodigies and reasoning to be recognized by people and be distinguishable from them by their relationship with Him. He then sent with them the Book to clarify His Legislation, and the scale of justice to set right all actions, and to observe discipline in all interactions so that double standards do not exist. He said in His Holy Quran: ***"Woe be to the deceivers; those who when they interact with people they take their due; but when they give by measure or by weight to them, they give less than is due"*** [83:1-3]. So the Messenger is the teacher of the decree of God Almighty for His creation in the way of worship. The Messenger, Muhammad (PBHH), has indeed clarified to the people this decree by saying to them: **"Religion is interaction with good conduct"**. This leaves no ground for any person to proclaim that the decree of God Almighty for humankind is for them to be faultless. Furthermore, Prophet Muhammad (PBHH), the conveyer of God's Message who does not speak out of his own accord (*"...nor does he (Muhammad) speak with any inclination (other than that of God Almighty)"* [53:3]) said: **"If it had not been in your nature to sin, God Almighty would have done away with you and would have created people who sin, and then seek His forgiveness, and hence God Almighty will grant them His forgiveness"**[1].

God Almighty also said in the Quran: *"Say: "O my I'bad (people) who have transgressed excessively upon themselves! Do not despair of the Mercy of God Almighty: for indeed God Almighty forgives all sins: It is He who is Ever-Forgiving, Most Merciful"* [39:53]. Thus the Message brought forth by every Prophet sent by God Almighty, shows that there are wrongdoings called *sins* and *evil deeds* and that He, Glory be to Him, will punish their doers in the hereafter. However, He may also forgive them because He described Himself as the All-Forgiving, Clement, Merciful, Pardoning and Forgiver of all sins. Furthermore, had God Almighty not forgiven them, and sent them to hell, the Prophet (PBHH) may save them from punishment by his intercession that is granted for the grave sinners of his followers. The Prophet (PBHH) said: **"My intercession is for the grave sinners of my** *Ummah (followers of* Muhammad in all religions)."**[2] God Almighty said: *"Those (the Jews and the Christians) unto whom We have sent the Revelation before it (the Quran) believe in it, and when it is recited to them they say we believe in it; verily, it is the Truth from our Lord; indeed, we have already been Muslims before this; those will receive their reward two-fold for their patience."* [28:52-54]

On the other hand, there are also righteous deeds, and their doer will be blessed in this life and rewarded in the hereafter by the Just, Ruling, Sovereign. The Message also clarifies that people are required to have good conduct and to do righteous deeds in order to be among those whom neither fear nor grief shall befall them. The Divine Legislation has elucidated the foundations for interaction between people by which they attain the Grace of God Almighty, and

---

[1] Sahih Muslim
[2] Sahih Ibn Habban

by which righteous communities are formed. He comprehensively included these Legislations in His Book which He revealed to His Messengers, and those who abide by them and follow the guidance of the Messenger are the best worshippers among people. God Almighty praised those worshippers and described them as: *"The worshippers of the Compassionate are those who tread on earth humbly, and when addressed by the non-appreciating, they respond with peace"* [25:63]. The believers are those who shun pride, who avoid the ignorant (about the essence of religion), who kneel earnestly in prayer, pray at night, appealing fervently to God Almighty to save them from the torment of Hell, who spend without being wasteful, who do not take the life of others, violating the sanctity given to life by God Almighty, and who avoid adultery, false testimonials, and frivolous speech, respecting God Almighty's verses, praying to Him to ameliorate their spouses and offspring and hoping to be exemplars among virtuous people. God Almighty promised those people a good ending and an eternal life filled with luxuries: *"Those are the ones who will be rewarded with the highest place in heaven because of their patient endurance. Therein they shall be received with salutations and peace, dwelling therein eternally – a beautiful place of rest and residence"* [25:75-6].

God Almighty also said, describing the members of the righteous community:

"Those who properly perform their prayer [70:23];
And those in whose wealth is a consigned right, for the pauper and the deprived [70:24-5];
And those who have faith in the Day of Judgement [70:26];
And those who are considerate of the Justice of their Lord – for the Justice of their Lord is unforeseen [70:27-8];
And those who guard their chastity, except with their spouses or those with whom they have an unofficial marriage where they are not to blame; and whosoever sought (to satisfy their desire) beyond this, those are the transgressors [70:29-31];
And those who guard what they have been entrusted with, and also their pledges [70:32];
And those who stand firm in their testimonies [70:33];
And those who uphold their prayer; those shall in heaven be

rewarded generously [70:34-35]. In fact, the aim of the Message is the formation of a righteous community where integrity of morals, love, and peace prevail.

Prophet Muhammad (PBHH) said: **"Smiling in your brother's face is an act of benevolence"[1]**, **"(the utterance of) a kind word is an act of benevolence"[2]**, and **"Charity quenches the Lord's wrath"[3]**. God Almighty also said: *"Surely, the Charitable men and women who give a benevolent loan to God Almighty (lend a bounteous contribution), shall be repaid manifold, and shall have a generous reward"* [57:18]. So, God Almighty considered people's charity as a debt on Him and a benevolent loan, multiplied manifold in return. Moreover, they shall have from Him other generous rewards. It is not the aim of the Message to demand from people to be free of sins, and to reject the sinners, degrade, defame and expose them. Protection (from exposure) is, in fact, one of the aims of Islam, as Prophet Muhammad says: **"Whoever protects a Muslim** (from being exposed), **God Almighty will protect him on the Day of Resurrection."[4]** Even if someone were to see with his own eyes a man having sexual intercourse with a woman who is not his wife, he shall be punished by being whipped eighty lashes if he speaks forth about it, without producing four witnesses; and further testimony (in court) on his part will henceforth not be accepted until he repents: *"And those who disgrace chaste women, and do not bring four eye witnesses, whip them eighty lashes; and do not accept their testimony at all - And those are the defilers,"* [24:4] *"Those who disgrace unsuspecting, chaste, women of faith, are condemned in this life and in the Hereafter, and shall have a grievous sufferance"* [24:23].

So, Islamic legislation has been most uncompromising regarding the protection of women and their rights amongst all legislations, to the extent that God Almighty condemned to damnation all those who slander women in this life and the Hereafter, and He promised them a grievous sufferance. Herein resides the secret to society's harmony. As

[1] Sunan Tirmithi
[2] Musnad Ahmad
[3] Sahih Ibn Habban
[4] Musnad Ahmad

16

for those who believe that a harmonious society is attained through spying on people's faults, prying on them and revealing their private affairs, and punishing them after their exposure, they should know that this is not Islam; such behaviour may be attributed to anything else but definitely not to Islam. On the contrary, Islam based society's harmony on protecting privacy, turning a blind eye to others' faults, and scolding and punishing those who pry on people's privacy. Once a man came to Prophet Muhammad (PBHH) in tears, mourning the deterioration of people's morals, presumptuously concerned for society's discipline, and said to him: "I saw a man having sexual intercourse with a woman, O Messenger of God Almighty". The Prophet (PBHH) gently rebuked him saying: **"It would have been more appropriate for you to shield them with your garment"[1]**. In fact, the Prophet (PBHH) is the most concerned for the welfare of people and their society, as attested to by God Almighty: *"(he is) exceedingly concerned for you..."* [9:228], *"The Prophet is the guardian of all people of faith, more so than their selves..."* [33:6]. In acknowledging women's distinct status, the Prophet (PBHH) said: **"Be good to women"[2]** , and: **"Whoever honours women is a noble person"[3]**, also: **"The best among you are those who are good to their women-folk"[4]**. God Almighty said: *"...and do not ill-treat them (women) to constrain them..."* [65:6] The Prophet (PBHH) also confirmed that: **"Paradise is at the feet of mothers"[5]** , as God Almighty said: *"...with sufferance his mother bore him, and with sufferance she gave birth to him..."* [46:15] Therefore, it does not stand to reason that the Prophet (PBHH) who said: **"From your world, women have been made beloved to me"[6]** should be referred to as the one who said that the majority of those in Hell are women[7]! In fact, he said: **"Women are the soul mates of men."[8]**

---

[1] Musnad Ahmad
[2] Sahih Muslim
[3] Kashf al Khafa'a
[4] Sunan Ibn Majah
[5] Al-Kamil Fi Doa'faa Al Rijal – That means that paradise is attained by treating mothers with respect and reverence
[6] Al Mustadrak Ala Al Sahihayn
[7] Sahih Muslim
[8] Sunan Tirmithi

17

If the aim of worship is the salvation and happiness of the worshippers in eternal life, then those who believe in the Messengers are those who adhere most to their Messages in order to achieve this happiness. But some people limited the concept of worship to the tight boundaries of physical acts like fasting, recitation of the Holy Quran, and night prayers, as if those comprise the essence of worship for being virtuous for a virtuous society. Whereas, worship embraces all of the human being's behaviours and actions as: **"Religion is interaction with good conduct"**. It is enough to refrain from causing harm to others to be described as a good Muslim in society, as the Prophet (PBHH) says: **"The Muslim is the one from whose harm - by hand or tongue - people are safe"**[1]. The "Muslim" here includes all Muslims of all faiths - Christianity, Judaism, and others.[2] God Almighty said: *"Verily, those who lower their voices before the Messenger of God Almighty, are indeed the ones whose hearts God Almighty has tested for piety: for them is Forgiveness and Great Reward."* [49:3] Here, the mere act of lowering one's voice has a great reward. God Almighty also stressed: *"... and lower your voice..."* [31:19]

The best deeds are those carried out for the sake of attaining the blessing of God Almighty. In fact, attaining this blessing in all religions is explicitly **"the Glorious Choice of God Almighty for humankind"** and it is that which the Messengers called for. *Jihad* (striving one's self towards attaining the blessing of God Almighty) is where a Muslim directs all his efforts and actions to achieve the Glorious Choice of God Almighty. It does not necessitate war and fighting. Thus, people who insist on holding steadfastly to what the Messengers brought forth and exhort themselves upon it, not caring for the hardship and opposition, until they are forced to leave their homeland, indeed such people are considered to be striving to attain the blessing of God Almighty, with their money and their selves. Being compelled to leave their homeland cannot be considered anything less than *Jihad*. God Almighty said: *"...if you have indeed departed your homes (Jihad) to attain my blessing..."*

---

[1] Sunan Al-Nasaa'i
[2] Muslims are the believers of their messengers – Muhammad (PBHH), Jesus, Moses, David, and other Messengers – Refer to the chapter on Islam

18

[60:1] Leaving one's home generally may or may not be *Jihad* (for the sake of attaining the blessing of God Almighty). However, in this context, it is *Jihad*, but it definitely does not mean fighting. In fact, *Jihad* is the apex and summit of worship one can perform, according to the Prophet's saying[1], and the greatest of it is *Jihadul Nafs:* striving to control one's self or one's own desires, which the Prophet (PBHH) has described as the greatest *Jihad.* Consequently, people who die striving to attain the blessing of God Almighty, even if in their bed, have died Martyrs, without fighting. The Prophet (PBHH) said: **"The majority of the martyrs in my** *Ummah* (followers of Prophet Muhammad (PBHH) in all religions) **are those who die in their deathbed, whereas one killed in the battle field, only God Almighty knows his intention."**[2]

---

[1] "Jihad is the apex of Islam" Sunan Tirmithi
[2] Musnad Ahmad

19

The Methodology of Preaching

T hose who rebuke the sinners with their cruel preaching are themselves in need of it. Prophet Muhammad (PBHH) said: **"Facilitate, do not complicate** (life)**; bring joyful tidings, do not repel."[1]**, and he also said: **"Make people love God Almighty, and make them lovable to Him, then He will love you"[2]**. This is because those who make mistakes need support and need to be reminded of His mercy. He does not ask them to be free of sins, but it is enough to seek His forgiveness once mistakes occur. This is the methodology of preaching which induces good character. In fact, rebuke and cruel preaching never create the righteous, faultless society, because this is an impossible thing so long as human beings remain human. The Prophet (PBHH) said: **"All the sons of Adam are predisposed to sin, and the best of the sinners are those who repeatedly repent"[3]**. Therefore, the most befitting act, instead of rebuke and cruel preaching, is to encourage people to do righteous deeds. When people's deeds become righteous, their wrongdoings decrease and their characters improve. Good character cannot be attained except when the person believes in the divine abstract

---

[1] Sahih Al-Bukhari
[2] Al Awliya'
[3] Al Mustadrak Ala Al Sahihayn

existence of God Almighty. If people reach this state of belief through the teacher (PBHH), then they will have faith in God Almighty and His Messenger. They will find themselves receiving and accepting all that the Prophet says, in accord with the saying of God Almighty: *"...nor does he (Muhammad) speak with any inclination (other than that of God Almighty)"* [53:3]. They will then realize that Prophet Muhammad (PBHH) has been sent to all people as a bearer of glad tidings, as a herald and as a teacher to them, but not as a ruler. The Messenger has but to deliver the Message of God Almighty, while the actual Ruler and King is God Almighty. Therefore, those who perceive the Message will then be constantly heedful of the presence of the omniscient God Almighty, the Supreme Ruler from whom nothing is concealed in the heavens or on Earth. So, how will this realization affect such individuals' dealings and behaviour? No doubt, they will be conscious of God Almighty the Ruler and King in every action they take, awaiting with great expectation their scale to become heavier on the Day of Judgement. Therefore, all their acts will be religious and the saying of the Prophet will befit them: **"Religion is interaction with good conduct".** They will be observing God Almighty in all their actions and seeking His blessing. They will be seeking to learn from the Prophet Muhammad (PBHH) how to obtain the blessing of God Almighty. Therefore, their seeking and behaviour would be in accordance with the Holy verse: *"...and whatever the Messenger consigns unto you, take it, and from whatever he forbids you, abstain..."* [59:7]. So, when they hear Prophet Muhammad (PBHH) say: **"Verily, I have been sent to perfect high moral qualities"** it will become clear to them that this is the true aim of the Message rather than secluding one's self in fasting, performing night prayers, and spiritual exercise, in order to acquire supernatural qualities like walking on water or fire, and flying. Those who acquire such qualities by which they can defy the rules of nature, and believe that this is the aim of the Message, have in fact, gone astray. This is because the aim of the Message is interaction with good conduct and not acquiring paranormal phenomena, which are not appropriate for preaching the Message in order to create a virtuous society. Moreover, the paranormal phenomena may lead to self-conceit and vanity, which is worse than sin. The Prophet (PBHH) said: **"If you**

did not sin, I would have feared for you what is worse than sin: self-conceit[1]. Those who acquire paranormal powers may think that by possessing these abilities they are secure from the unforeseen Justice of God Almighty. Such persons who are keen and persistent in these pursuits, with the intention of meeting God Almighty with their presumed perfect acts, aim at being secure from this unforeseen Justice, thereby losing their purpose in this life and the hereafter: *"...in fact none regard themselves to be secure from the unforeseen Justice of God Almighty except the losers"* [7:99]. Preaching through the use of supernatural abilities will not achieve any results, and it is not in conformity with Prophet Muhammad's Message:*"...and We have not sent (Muhammad) with signs (miracles) for the fact that former people have denied them..."* [17:59].

The miracles of Prophet Muhammad (PBHH) are innumerable and surpassed all the special miracles of the previous Messengers, amongst whom one has brought the dead back to life and created from mud a creature that can fly. Prophet Muhammad (PBHH) has in fact been endowed with the miracle of bringing things into existence from nothing, which no previous Prophet has been endowed with, as he once fed to satisfaction a whole army with two handfuls of barley. This means that a blessing and an increment had occurred to this amount of barley to become ample enough to feed an army, because it is impossible to feed more than ten persons with such an amount. Jesus, peace be upon him, who created from mud a resemblance of a bird, has created it from elements (water and earth) which he did not originally create but were already created by God Almighty, The Best of Creators. The Holy Quran cites Jesus saying: *"... I create for you from mud in the form of a bird, and then breathe into it hence it becomes a flying creature with the permission of God Almighty..."* [3:49]. As for satiating the hunger of more than ten persons, let alone an army of more than a thousand or thousands, by two handfuls of barley, this is beyond possibility and cannot be accounted for without the occurrence of a miracle of creating barley sufficient to feed that number. Prophet Muhammad (PBHH) has also been endowed with other miracles such as returning a ruptured eye

---

[1] Majma' al Zawa'id

23

back to its place, replacing an amputated limb, knowing who is in Heaven and who is in Hell, who will live to see certain events, causing the sun to move backwards in the sky after sunset, splitting the moon, and many others. In spite of all those previously mentioned miracles, they were not the core of the Message he was sent to deliver. God Almighty said: *"... and We have not sent (Muhammad) with signs (miracles) for the fact that former people have denied them..."* [17:59] Prophet Muhammad (PBHH) confirmed: **"Verily, I have been sent to perfect high moral qualities"[1].** He also said: **"The Muslim is the one from whose harm – by tongue or hand - people are safe"[2], "The person of faith is the one whom people trust"[3],** and: **"Whoever believes in God Almighty and the Day After is expected to speak good or remain silent."[4]** Also, in denouncing prejudice and partisanship, Prophet Muhammad (PBHH) says: **"Renounce it; for indeed, it stinks"[5]** since, with partisanship, brotherhood does not exist in society. In fact, Islam, the all-embracing Message, is all about the realisation of this brotherhood between people, since: **"A Muslim is the sibling of a Muslim, they neither fail nor oppress each other"[6],** and **"Muslims in their compassion and mercy towards each other are like one body, if one part is ill, the rest of the body will join in the suffering by fever and lack of sleep"[7].** We should not disregard the fact that Prophet Muhammad (PBHH) was sent to all humankind. Therefore, his address is to Muslims universally in all religions.

All the Messengers of God Almighty came to reform people, but it was necessary for every Messenger to enlighten his followers about the Divine abstract existence of God Almighty, which is the call for humankind to unify through monotheism: *"There is one God: only God Almighty"*. So, when a Messenger achieves this, he will have the obedience of his people who will then accede to him

---

[1] Musnad Ahmad
[2] Sahih Al-Bukhari
[3] Sahih Ibn Habban
[4] Sahih Muslim
[5] Sahih Al-Bukhari
[6] Sahih Al-Bukhari
[7] Sahih Muslim

and become Muslims, because they have faith in him as The Messenger of God Almighty. Hence, he will instruct them with what is necessary to better their conditions in this world and the Hereafter. The Almighty said: *"And We have made them (the Messengers) standard models, enlightening (people) with Our permission. And We have inspired them to do good deeds, perform prayers, and give Zakat (alms); and indeed they were worshippers of Us"* [21:73]. So, the Messengers of God Almighty enlightened people about the existence of the one God: *"There is one God: only God Almighty"*, and this exemplifies the oneness of the Message. Furthermore, they inspired them to do righteous deeds in order to create a virtuous society.

Islam

All Messengers, as previously mentioned, have been sent by God Almighty with religion which is Islam: *"...we do not differentiate between any of His Messengers..."* [2:285], because He said: *"Indeed, the religion to God Almighty is Islam."* [3:19]. Therefore, all the Messengers of the heavenly religions are Muslims. Abraham, peace be upon him, was a Muslim and was not of those who associate partners with God Almighty: *"...so Abraham consigned unto his sons (to be Muslims), and so did Jacob (saying:) "my sons, indeed, God Almighty has assigned this religion for you (all), then, do not die except as Muslims." "* [2:132]

The followers of Jesus (Peace Be Upon him) also confirm that they are Muslims: *"The disciples said: "We are the apostles of God. We have faith in God Almighty and attest that we are Muslims"* [3:52].

And Noah (Peace Be Upon him) said:

"...my reward is only from God Almighty, and I have been commanded to be a Muslim" [10:72].

"And Moses said (to the Jews): "O my people, if you have faith in God Almighty, then rely on Him, if indeed you are Muslims" [10:84].

Then came the saying of God Almighty:

"Abraham was neither a Jew nor a Christian, but was bonded to the all-embracing Islam, and he was not of those who associate partners with God Almighty" [3:67]. In spite of the fact that

27

Abraham preceded Christianity and Judaism, God Almighty described him as belonging to neither - Why has this obvious point been asserted with such strength? Negating his belonging to either religion, although he preceded them, is an emphasis on the call on people to prohibit partisanship into the confines of sects, and to prevent disintegration of the unity under the umbrella of the all-embracing Islam that has been brought forth by all Messengers, including Abraham, the father of Messengers: *"...and do not be of those who associate partners with God Almighty, of those who have disintegrated the unity of their religion and became sects, every sect rejoicing in what they believe"* [30:31-2].

In fact, Judaism, Christianity, and Sabianism are subtitles under the umbrella of the all-embracing Islam, similar to *Shiites* and *Sunnis* in the religion of Muhammad (PBHH), and Catholics and Protestants in the religion of Jesus, Peace be upon him, and all of them are Muslims. Thus, the all-embracing Islam is not confined to Judaism, Christianity, or Sabianism. That is to say, it is inappropriate for a Jew to confine the all-embracing Islam to Judaism only, or for a Christian to do likewise, but in fact some did: *"And they say, "Be Jews or Christians (so) you will become enlightened." Say (Muhammad), "Instead, (we follow) the religion of Abraham, a Muslim bonded to the all-embracing Islam and not of those who associate partners with God Almighty""* [2:135]. In fact, each of them was biased towards his belief: *"And never will the Jews and the Christians accept you unless you follow their religious sects"* [2:120]. They have become fanatically adherent to their respective religious sects, and so refused to accept God Almighty sending whoever He pleases to whomever he pleases. In addition, they envisage that there is no religion like theirs. God Almighty said: *"O People of the Book! Do not be unrightfully excessive in your religion..."* [4:171] This unrightful excessiveness and extremism is what prevents them from coexisting with other religions under the wide umbrella of the all-embracing Islam. Therefore, Prophet Muhammad (PBHH) was sent as the final Messenger to reveal freedom of faith and religion, and to clarify the scope of the all-embracing Islam that encompasses all religions without the fanaticism practiced by some of the followers of the Holy books and by those who are ignorant amongst his followers. God Almighty said: *"The Jews say, "The Christians are*

28

unto nothing (of the truth)" and the Christians say, "The Jews are unto nothing (of the truth)" in spite of the fact that they (both) recite the Book. Likewise, those who have no knowledge (the ignorant amongst the followers of Prophet Muhammad) say the same..." [2:113]. Therefore, it is more providential for the Jews not to deny Christianity and for the Christians not to deny Judaism, and for both of them not to look with arrogance and discontent at the followers of Prophet Muhammad (PBHH). The followers of Prophet Muhammad (PBHH) should also not deny the previous religions of Judaism and Christianity; otherwise, they will be like them and the verse *"Likewise, those who have no knowledge say the same..."* [2:113] would befit them. Saying that the Christians are unto nothing and the Jews are unto nothing is, in fact, wronging other religions that have been sent by God Almighty which are all Islam. It is beyond the realm of reason for God Almighty to send a faulty religion, for He is above sending it faulty or incomplete, as everything that comes from Him is absolute perfection. All Glory and Praise be to God Almighty who sent all His Messengers with the perfect wholesome Message of Islam: *"Say (followers of Muhammad) "We have faith in God Almighty and in that which is revealed unto us; and in that which was revealed unto Abraham, Ishmael, Isaac, Jacob and his sons (the Tribes), and that which was given to Moses, Jesus and the other Prophets from their Lord. We do not differentiate between any of them (as Messengers of God Almighty), and to Him (God Almighty) we are Muslims (surrendering ourselves)"* [2:136]. God Almighty has concluded their succession with His beloved Prophet Muhammad (PBHH) in order to clarify for all the people what has been sent to them: *"...and We have sent you the Revelation (O Muhammad) to clarify to people what has been sent to them"* [16:44] and to clear away and rectify any deviation which had been incurred by the people upon the former religions. He also said: *"O people of the Book! Our Messenger has come to you, revealing and clarifying to you much of what you have concealed of the Book, and of much, he is most pardoning. There has come to you from God Almighty a Light (Muhammad) and an enlightening Book"* [5:15]. Therefore, no one should ascribe incompleteness to God Almighty's religion that had been sent to the Jews and the Christians, challenging the perfection

29

of His actions. So, Prophet Muhammad (PBHH) came with his Message *"...confirming the Books that came before it, and embracing them..."* [5:48] and removing the fanatical religious attitudes of some Jews and Christians who reject any religion other than their own. He founded the principle of freedom of religion: that no compulsion should exist in matters of faith and interaction; and he approved all former religions sent by God Almighty. Hence, he established the freedom of faith, which, if viewed without partisanship, is the all-embracing Islam. Every religion that came from God Almighty is the Truth, as He said: *"If they had effected the Torah and the Injeel (Bible) and that which was revealed unto them from their Lord, they would have certainly enjoyed abundance from above and from underfoot."* [5:66] He also said: *"Indeed, We have sent the Torah, wherein there is guidance and light, by which all the Prophets who have submitted (to God Almighty) adjudicate to those who sought enlightenment..."* [5:44]. So, the followers of all religions within the realm of the all-embracing Islam - the followers of Muhammad, the Christians, the Jews, and the Sabians - are member parties under its vast and all-embracing umbrella. They shall have their reward from their Lord and neither fear nor grief shall befall them, if they fulfil the conditions of having faith in God Almighty and the Day After, and doing the righteous deed, which is good conduct, since **"Religion is interaction with good conduct"**.

The knowledge that all religions which came from God Almighty are Islam, and are the Truth, dispels the bias of all people towards their Book and their religion. This bias is the partisanship about which Prophet Muhammad (PBHH) said: **"Renounce it; for indeed, it stinks"[1]**. This knowledge is indeed the foundation of faith tolerance with which good conduct is achieved between religions. In fact, the bias of the Jews to their religion led to their loss of the privilege which God Almighty had bestowed upon them, as He stated in the Holy Quran: *"And We have indeed given the Children of Israel the Book, the Authority of Law, Prophethood, and We have bestowed upon them pure provisions, favoured them over others, and provided them with sound enlightenment from the*

---

[1] Sahih Al-Bukhari

30

realm of Divine Order" [45:16-17]. Accordingly, they thought highly of themselves to the extent that they rejected other religions and felt superior to others: *"And they did not become sects except after the knowledge (the advent of Prophet Muhammad) - an act of injustice between themselves"* [45:17]. Even this dissention should be left to God Almighty to deal with, since people should not be persecuted for their faith nor be forced to leave it and embrace another: *"Indeed, your Lord will judge between them on the Day of Resurrection on their dissention"* [45:17].

Likewise, many of the Arabs believe that Prophet Muhammad (PBHH) is their own Prophet and not the universal Messenger for all people. Since his Message embraces and approves all preceding religions, they believe themselves to be better than the former nations, not recognizing that there is no privilege in their being Arabs. The true privilege, however, is in being followers of Prophet Muhammad (society of Muslims in all religions) where there is no privilege for an Arab over a non-Arab, nor for a white person over a black one, except by heedfulness of God Almighty. Most of them misunderstood the saying of God Almighty: *"You were the best society brought forth for humankind..."* [3:110] by thinking that the society of Prophet Muhammad (PBHH) were the Arabs only, despite the fact that the Prophet (PBHH) has made it very clear that there is no privilege for Arabs over others except by heedfulness of God Almighty. Therefore, whoever believes otherwise should reflect on the words of God Almighty: *"The Arabs are the worst in disbelief and hypocrisy, and most worthy of not knowing the limits of what has been revealed by God Almighty to His Messenger (Muhammad)..."* [9:97] and His saying: *"And among the Arabs around you are hypocrites, and from the residents of Medina are those who have perfected the practice of hypocrisy"* [9:101], and His saying: *"The Arabs said, "We have Faith". Say (to them), you do not have Faith; but you should say "we have surrendered (become Muslims)"; as Faith has yet to enter your hearts"* [49:14]. So, the society of Prophet Muhammad (PBHH) are the Muslims from all races and all religions: *"We have not sent you (O Muhammad) but as a universal Messenger to all people"* [34:28]. Regarding their ethnic origin, all Arabs, Jews, and Christians belong to Adam, and Adam is from dust; thus clarified Muhammad the

31

Prophet of Mercy (PBHH). The society of Prophet Muhammad (PBHH) is the best community brought forth for people because it embraces Muslims in all religions. Therefore, the Book of Prophet Muhammad (PBHH) has come endorsing and embracing all the Messages before it, and not rejecting them. It was the criterion[1] and the principal reference that embraced them all. God Almighty has sent this Book to His Beloved Prophet, Muhammad (PBHH), *"to proclaim his transcendence over all religion"* [9:33] with his high moral qualities, his establishment of faith tolerance, freedom of thought, and freedom of faith.

---

[1] (as mentioned in the Holy Quran in verse [25:1])

How to Preach
the Message

To call for knowing God Almighty is the base from which all Messengers start the reformation to create virtuous societies that have high moral qualities. After believing in God Almighty, comes having faith in His Prophet: *"O believers, be heedful of God Almighty and have faith in his Messenger..."* [57:28], who conveys the Divine Legislation from Him, and is thus obeyed: *"And We have not sent forth a Messenger but (for him) to be obeyed in accordance with the Will of God Almighty."* [4:64] Henceforth, the Messenger establishes the teachings that refine society in order to perfect high moral qualities.

A poet[1] said:

Teach youngsters the knowledge that shows them
The ways of life, but before that teach them manners

Another poet[2] said:

Nations with good manners prevail

---

[1] Mohammed Saeed Al-Abbasy
[2] Ahmed Shawqy

Once their good manners are lost, then perish they shall

The manners that religions call for commence with respect for the people, for whose sake the Message of God Almighty has been delivered. The Creator thus honours them, so that the Prophet's methodology may come in harmony with this honouring. God Almighty said: *"We have honoured the children of Adam"* [17:70]. He then favoured them above many of His creation: *"...and we have favoured them much more than many of our creation"* [17:70]. Prophet Muhammad asserted the honoured status of the human being as he said: **"Human beings are dependant on God Almighty, and the most beloved to Him are those who benefit them most."**[1]. Imam Ali said that people are of two kinds: **"Your brother in religion or your equal in creation."** God Almighty said: *"O people! We have created you from a male and a female, and made you into nations and tribes, that you may know each other. Verily the most honoured of you in the view of God Almighty is (the one who is) the most heedful of you. And God Almighty is All-Knowing and All-Aware."* [49:13]. The Prophet Muhammad (PBHH) also said: **"There is no merit for an Arab over a non-Arab, nor for a white person over a black person except through piety."**[2]. The apex of good manners is piety which cannot be an attribute of hypocrites, criminals, immoral persons, or liars. It describes those who do not inflict harm on others and whose goodness surpasses them. Such persons are those who devote all their efforts towards reform with the Prophet (PBHH) as their guiding standard.

The reform of the human being is indeed the aim of the Message: **"If God Almighty guides one person through you, it is better for you than to have the best of wealth."**[3] Prophet Muhammad once looked at the *Kaaba* (in *Makkah*) and said: **"How wonderful you are and how wonderful is your scent, how grand you are and how grand is your sacredness. By the One in whose Hand Muhammad's life is, the sacredness of a believer is even grander**

---

[1] Al Mo'gam Al Kabeer
[2] Fateh Al Barey
[3] Sahih Al-Bukhari

34

than yours."[1] Thus, Prophets were sent by God Almighty with the Message to reform human beings until they become spiritually greater than the sacredness of the *Kaaba* and the angels. Some people might misinterpret the following verse of the Holy Quran and think that the angels are better than Jesus: *"Neither Christ will disdain being a worshipper of God Almighty, nor shall the closest angels"* [4:172]. What is implied in this verse is not the favouring of the angels over Jesus, the Soul of God Almighty and son of Mary. Rather, the verse stresses the fact that they are all worshippers of God Almighty. In spite of the fact that Jesus was born only to a mother (without a biological father), he will not abstain from worshipping God Almighty, nor shall the angels who have neither a mother nor a father.

The refinement of humankind is the purpose of sending all Messengers with the Message. Accordingly, the methodology of Prophet Muhammad (PBHH) was totally devoid of any trace of harshness or cruelty, for he was created free of them. He was the example of Divine Perfection, *"...and a luminous source of light"* [33:46]. God Almighty says: *"Had you (O Muhammad) been harsh or hard-hearted, they would have left you..."* [3:159]. If a certain situation required sternness, he would then be ordered by God Almighty to be stern, because his manners were entirely devoid of it: *"O Prophet! Strive hard against the opposers and the hypocrites, and be stern with them."* [9:73]. He was thus praised by his Creator for having high moral qualities. Striving *(Jihad)* here means to contend with firm words and sound argument, and does not mean using the sword. This has been clearly illustrated by the use of the command to strive *(Jihad)* against the opposers and the hypocrites together; a fact which excludes the call for war, since war cannot be waged against hypocrites who exist amongst the queues of the Muslims and cannot be singled out. Prophet Muhammad (PBHH) said: **"There are twelve hypocrites amongst my companions; eight of them shall never enter Paradise until the camel passes through the eye of a needle."**[2] So, striving *(Jihad)* against them can only mean the use of firm words of warning, because firmness is

---

[1] Sunan Ibn Majah
[2] Sahih Muslim

35

used as an adjective to describe words, not to describe war. Thus, the Prophet (PBHH) would become a herald to them and a foreteller of painful suffering: *"...foretell them of painful suffering"* [3:21], a warning which befits both the opposers and the hypocrites. The bearing of glad tidings is for those who have faith, even if their foot slips by a major sin. The Prophet Muhammad (PBHH) says: **"Whoever commits a sin and realises that God Almighty is aware of his deed will be forgiven even if he does not ask for forgiveness"**[1] because the believers who sin are better than the hypocrites. Prophet Muhammad (PBHH) also said: **"A worshipper committed a sin and said 'God Almighty I have sinned, please forgive me' so God Almighty will say 'My worshipper knows that he has a God who might forgive sins or punish for them. I have forgiven my worshipper.' Then after a while he sinned again and said 'I have sinned once more; please forgive me' so God Almighty will say 'My worshipper has learnt that he has a God who might forgive sins or punish for them. I have forgiven my worshipper.' Then after a while he commits another sin and for the third time says 'I have sinned, so forgive me.' God Almighty will say 'My worshipper has learnt that he has a God who might forgive sins or punish for them. I have forgiven my worshipper three times; he is to do what he desires'."**[2]

Striving *(Jihad)* with words is more powerful than striving with the sword because the effect of the word is more profound on the addressees and is more pronounced than that of the sword. A sword ends life, but words endure so long as life continues. The sword and wars were not used to force people into Islam during the life of Prophet Muhammad (PBHH). The battle of *Badr* was aimed at the trade caravan of the opposers from the tribe of *Quraysh,* in order to recompense the losses of the immigrants who were unjustly forced out of their homes. It was *Quraysh* who had insisted on going to war after their trade caravan was secured as they had wanted to flaunt their strength and to humiliate Muslims in their own land. The battle of *Uhud* was in defence of the city of *Medina* against the opposers who had attacked it, and the battle of *Al Ahzab* had also been a

[1] Sahih Al-Bukhari
[2] Sahih Al-Bukhari

defensive response to an attack by the enemies on the *Medina*. So, Prophet Muhammad (PBHH) in all these battles was on the defensive.

As for the conquest of *Makkah* , it was not a war in the known sense. Not a single person was killed or taken prisoner, but in fact, the Prophet Muhammad (PBHH) said: **"O God Almighty, I am not responsible for what Khalid Ibn Al Waleed has done"**[1] because Khaled had killed some of the opposers he had encountered upon entering *Makkah.* No women were enslaved, and there was no looting, and neither did Prophet Muhammad (PBHH) appoint a governor over *Makkah to* collect taxes. Above all, he did not order them to proclaim that there is no God but God Almighty, and did not force anyone to proclaim that he, Muhammad, is the Messenger of God Almighty. The wars of the Prophet Muhammad (PBHH) were only carried out in self defence. God Almighty does not love transgression, even if it were for the sake of spreading the Message: *"There is no compulsion in religion..."* [2:256], *"...will you then compel people, against their will, to believe!"* [10:99]. If compulsion has any place in the methodology of Islam, then the first thing the people of *Makkah* would have been asked to do after the conquest would be to convert to Islam.

The following saying that is claimed to have been said by Prophet Muhammad (PBHH) contradicts his methodology: **"I was ordered to battle with people until they say there is no God but God Almighty. Once they say that, their life and wealth are safe from me and their judgement is left to God Almighty."**[2] This saying also contradicts the saying of God Almighty: *"Invite (O Muhammad) (all) towards attaining the blessing of your Lord with wisdom and beautiful preaching; and debate with them in ways that are best and most gracious"* [16:125]. It is impossible that a saying would come from Prophet Muhammad (PBHH) to contradict the Holy Quran. The source from which this saying has been taken is not faultless; therefore this is to be taken into consideration as to the authenticity of the saying. Furthermore, God Almighty said: *"And do not debate with the People of the Book, except with the best and*

---

[1] Sahih Al-Bukhari
[2] Musnad Ahmad

most gracious means..." [29:46] because spreading the Message among those who are not Muslims is accomplished through wisdom and good sermons. However, among Muslims in all religions, there is no need to preach the Message; but the aim is to reform the conduct, since they are already Muslims. If the ungracious sermon is forbidden in calling non-Muslims to Islam, then for Muslims in all religions it is absolutely prohibited: **"Death suffices as a reminder"**[1]. The way to preach has been defined by God Almighty in the Holy Quran, and Prophet Muhammad (PBHH) has established it in his methodology, and no other person has the authority to change this methodology. Prophet Muhammad (PBHH) said: **"Make people love God Almighty, and make them lovable to Him, then He will love you"**[2], and he said: **"Facilitate, do not complicate** (life); **bring joyful tidings, do not repel."**[3]

Violence was never a method for spreading the Message. This was made clear in the conquest of *Makkah*. The aim behind the conquest was to break down the dominance of the leaders who opposed the preaching of the forbearance of Islam, forbade the freedom of thought and would not tolerate others' rights to portray different values and ideas. God Almighty says: *"Fight the chief opposers who have no faith; they do not abide by their oaths"* [9:12] because they are the ones who control and influence their people and forbid them from listening to other opinions, thereby repressing the freedom of thought. Therefore, conquering *Makkah* was not in order to enforce a certain opinion or religion. Rather, it was to liberate the people of *Makkah* from the oppressive regime which was averse to, and violent towards all new beliefs, and forms of freedom of thought.

The conquest of *Makkah* sets a clear example of why and how war is waged in Islam. The purpose of the conquest was not to impose a religion on people, as Prophet Muhammad (PBHH) did not ask the people of *Makkah* to proclaim that there is no God but God Almighty; instead, he left them free to think and believe as they wished. He made Islam lovable to them so they would embrace it

---

[1] Majma' al-Zawa'id
[2] Al-Awliya'
[3] Sahih Al-Bukhari

willingly, and he used to give some of the non-believers who listened to him like Abu Sofian a portion from the *Zakat* (alms) money. The Prophet Muhammad (PBHH) would not have waged war against them if they had allowed freedom of thought and had not violated the truce[1] and had not interfered with people's freedom of choice. God Almighty said: *"Whoever desires to believe can do so, and whoever desires to reject is free to do so"* [18:29] because this is what the Message advocated, in clear contrast and contradiction to the attitude of tyrannical rulers. God Almighty also said: *"If you were to be put in authority, would you then do mischief in the land and break your ties of kith and kin? Such are the people whom God Almighty has cursed"* [47:22-23]. Tyranny was the reason why God Almighty had sent Prophet Moses (PBUH) to the Pharaoh of Egypt: *"Go to the Pharaoh, for he had indeed transgressed all bounds."* [20:24]

Therefore, waging wars had never been a methodology of preaching Islam. No killing took place in the conquest of *Makkah.* If war is forced upon Muslims, then they would have to defend themselves, but if the enemy then calls for peace, even if the Muslims felt that victory was on their side, they should comply, as God Almighty says: *"But if the enemy inclines towards peace, you too incline towards it"* [8:61]. The methodology of Islam extends to honourable dealings with the enemies who do not attempt to fight, as God Almighty said: *"God Almighty does not forbid you from dealing kindly and honourably with those who did not fight you for (your) faith and did not drive you out of your homes: Verily, God Almighty loves those who are honourable."* [60:8]

---

[1] Al-Hudaybiya treaty of peace

Legislation

I n general, laws are meant to organize social relationships and to regulate dealings. The legislations of Prophet Muhammad (PBHH) came holistic: including both the laws in the Torah and the tolerance in the Bible. God Almighty says: *"...confirming the Books that came before it, and embracing them"* [5:48].

The aim of legislation in the Message of Prophet Muhammad is to refine people and raise them from a life of ignorance to transcendent manners, at the apex of which Prophet Muhammad (PBHH), whom God Almighty has praised, is enthroned: *"...to proclaim his transcendence over all religion"* [48:28]. So he thus remains the source and the teacher of this Message and of all Messages that constitute the religion to God Almighty. From him are to be taken the principles of these Messages and the methodology of preaching and spreading them, as God Almighty says: *"We have not sent you (O Muhammad) but as a universal Messenger to all people"* [34:28].

God Almighty began with the family - the nucleus of society: *"And We have consigned the human being to be kind to his/her parents: with sufferance his/her mother bore him/her, and with sufferance she gave birth to him/her."* [46:15]. So, God Almighty defined the boundaries of dealing with parents: *"...do not say to them 'uff' ('humph') ..."* [17:23] which is the least utterance a person makes which shows how sacred the parents are. He added *"...nor scold them"* [17:23], which includes not raising one's voice. He also

41

made it a duty to pray for them: *"... and say: "My Lord, have mercy on them as they have cherished me in childhood.""* [17:24] He said: *"Your Lord has decreed that you worship none but Him, and that you be gentle in dealing with parents. Whether one or both of them attain old age in life, do not say to them 'uff' ('humph'), nor scold them, but address them honourably and, out of mercy and kindness be humble in dealing with them, and say: "My Lord have mercy on them as they have cherished me in childhood. "* [17:23-4]

After having faith in God Almighty and in His Prophet (PBHH) comes attentiveness to the family: *"Say: "Behold, I will recite what your Lord has prohibited you from": do not associate anything as partner with Him; and be gentle in dealing with parents"* [6:151].

Subsequent to attentiveness to the parents, God Almighty urges people to be benevolent and give attention to: *"...kinsfolk, orphans, those in need, neighbours who are kin, neighbours who are near, the companion in need, the wayfarer (you meet), and those who are affiliated to you"* [4:36]. To whomever does not respond to this ordainment, by dealing benevolently with them, God Almighty says: *"Verily, God Almighty does not love the arrogant, the vainglorious: those who act niggardly, and enjoin niggardliness on others, and hide what God Almighty has bestowed upon them from His bounty"* [4:36-37]. Those who refuse to acknowledge the Grace of God Almighty upon them and conceal the blessing which He has bestowed upon them are in fact deniers and ungrateful to His blessing: *"And We have prepared, for those who are ungrateful, a humiliating sufferance"* [4:37]. Though God Almighty warns against miserliness He also warns against extravagance: *"and do not squander your wealth in the manner of a spendthrift. Verily spendthrifts are brothers of the devils and the devil is ungrateful to his Lord"* [17:26-27]. Then He warns against killing one's children out of fear of poverty: *"Do not kill your children for reason of deprivation – We shall provide sustenance for you and for them –"* [6:151], which exemplifies heedfulness to the rights of children.

The establishment of rules regulating the conduct of society continues: *"...abstain from shameful deeds, whether publicly or privately..."* [6:151].

The Lawgiver also stresses the importance of preservation of human life: *"Do not take the life, which God Almighty has made sacred, except by way of justice and law."* [6:151]. The sanctity given to life by God Almighty is such that if one kills a single person wrongfully, it will be like killing all people, as He said: *"Anyone who kills a person – unless it be legal punishment for murder or for spreading mischief in the land – it would be as if he had killed all people."* [5:32].

He also made it imperative to manage the wealth of orphans or those who have not come of age with prudence: *"Do not attempt to manage an orphan's wealth except with honour and prudence, until they attain the age of maturity..."* [6:152].

Then He clarifies the way to interact commercially: *"...and give due measure and weight with equity – We do not assign unto any soul, but that which it can bear –"* [6:152].

Then God Almighty addressed observing truthfulness in speech: *"... if you give your word, be fair even if it is against a kinsperson..."* [6:153] as a Muslim is expected to speak only the truth. Prophet Muhammad (PBHH) had been asked if a believer lies and he said: **"No"** and he recited the saying of God Almighty: *"Verily, it is the non-believers who make up lies..."* [16:105].

Then follows fulfilling one's pledged promise: *"And fulfil the promises you make under the name of God Almighty: He has thus entrusted you, that you may be heedful"* [6:152].

The Lawgiver demands taking great care in handling news: *"O believers, if a depraved person comes to you with any news, ascertain the truth, lest you harm people unwittingly, and afterwards become full of repentance for what you have done."* [49:6].

He orders people to promote peace between inimical parties, even if this necessitates enforcing peace upon the perpetrator, as the following verse reveals: *"If two parties among the believers fall into dispute, make peace between them: but if one of them then transgresses against the other, then fight against the one that transgresses until it complies with the Divine Order (Legislation); if it complies, then make peace between them with justice, and be fair: For God Almighty loves those who are fair."* [49:9].

Establishing Divine Legislation (that maintains the God-given right of everyone) is indeed the aim of reconciliation and of termination of disputes in Islam. God Almighty has ordered that His

Divine Legislation be carried out under all circumstances and in all situations (even if transgression continues from a weakened opponent). He said:

"...And the belittling of others (to you) should not drive you away from being just" [5:8],

"Verily, the believers are brothers: So make peace between your brothers; and be heedful of God Almighty, that you may receive mercy." [49:10],

"O believers, no group of people should mock another group, as they might be better than them" [49:11],

"...nor should women mock other women, as they might be better than them" [49:11],

"...and do not scorn or slander each other" [49:11],

"...and do not call each other by offensive names: Heinous is the wicked name-calling after belief: And those who do not repent are indeed the transgressors." [49:11],

"O believers avoid much of suspicion: for suspicion in some cases is a sin" [49:12],

"...and do not spy ..." [49:12],
"...nor backbite one another. Would one of you like to eat the flesh of one's own dead brother? You would then abhor this" [49:12],

"And do not endorse that which has not come to your knowledge; for every act of hearing, or of seeing, or of perception in the heart will be enquired into" [17:36],

"Do not tread on earth flamboyantly; for you cannot penetrate the earth (by your weight), nor attain the height of mountains (in size)." [17:37],

"Do not undervalue people's possessions" [26:183],

"...and do not act wickedly on Earth, spreading corruption" [26:183].

These legislations in the Message of Prophet Muhammad (PBHH) are in effect subsumptive of all Messages, as he has endorsed them, saying: **"I am the institution of knowledge and Ali is its portal"**[1]. Therefore, it is not to be expected that those who have faith in Prophet Muhammad (PBHH) should act with aversion towards the believers in other religions. However, some Muslims in the nation of Prophet Muhammad (PBHH) are seen to be strongly averse to the followers of other religions and sometimes even to their Messengers. Their aversion has reached such a point where there is a noticeable lack of manners with respect to Jesus, Peace be upon him, who is the Soul of God Almighty. They might even interact with animosity towards those who glorify him, as if those persons no longer belong to the nation of Prophet Muhammad (PBHH). The divinity of God Almighty precludes that He deliver religions that are faulty, such that He tries to amend them in a succeeding Message. Every religion that came from God Almighty is the Islam which all Prophets have brought forth: *"We do not differentiate between any of His Messengers."* [2:285]. God Almighty says: *"And those who believe in God Almighty and His Messengers and do not differentiate between any of them, He shall give them their rewards: For God Almighty is Oft-Forgiving, Most Merciful."* [4:152]. Hence: *"The religion to God Almighty is Islam"* [3:19]. However, some followers of the Prophets of those religions have distorted the meanings of the words of God Almighty according to their desire. Such an act of distortion is unacceptable. Prophet Muhammad (PBHH) had foreseen for his nation that: **"You will follow the ways of those who came before you span by span and cubit by cubit**[2]**; even if they entered a lizard's hole you would follow them."**[3] This means that the followers of Prophet Muhammad

---

[1] Tahzeeb Al Tahzeeb
[2] The span *(shibr)* and cubit *(dhira'a)* were used to measure distances
[3] Sahih Al-Bukhari

45

(PBHH) too would distort the meanings in his religion, as those before them had done, and in fact they have.

Dear Muslim follower of Muhammad (PBHH), you should not feel embarrassed to show respect and sanctification to Jesus, Peace be upon him, the Soul of God Almighty, despite what the ignorant others say. Some of those who claim to be knowledgeable think that the following of Prophet Muhammad (PBHH) entails hating other Prophets. Whereas, it is their duty to respect other Prophets and hold them sacred. Otherwise, it is feared that you may be one of those who will not believe in Jesus, Peace be upon him, when he reappears and reigns over the world, if you live until the time of his reappearance - a fact which some Muslims in Muhammad's nation deny. Some of them think we are still far away from that time, while we see that it is soon: *"And of the People of the Book there shall be some who will indeed believe in him (Jesus) before his death; And on the Day of Judgement he will be a witness to them"* [4:159], *"And he (Jesus) is indeed a sign for the Day of Judgement"* [43:61].

How would you feel - you who have been informed by Prophet Muhammad (PBHH) about the reappearance of Jesus, Peace be upon him, as a just ruler at the end of time - if you found that the believers in other religions have outpaced you in believing in him? God Almighty said: *"And there are, certainly, among the People of the Book, those who believe in God Almighty, and in that which has been revealed unto you, and in that which has been revealed unto them, solemnly obeisant to God Almighty: They will not trade the verses of God Almighty for a little gain. For them is a reward with their Lord; indeed God Almighty is swift in retribution."* [3:199] God Almighty also said: *"Those whom We have given the Book rejoice at what has been revealed unto you; but some factions deny part of it."* [13:36]. Do not place yourself among these factions and become one of the deniers. To degrade the previous religions is to degrade the Prophets who delivered them. While this is clearly lack of honourable manners, it, moreover, constitutes disbelief in the Message of Prophet Muhammad (PBHH). The person who defames previous Messages is in fact questioning the truthfulness of the Message of Prophet Muhammad (PBHH), as God Almighty said that it came: *"...confirming the Books that came before it, and*

46

embracing them..." [5:48] and *"...then comes to you a Messenger, confirming what you have (of the Book)..."* [3:81].

To believe in the previous Messages is in fact a confirmation of the truthfulness of Prophet Muhammad (PBHH). The Truth in them should be held in deep reverence. *"...And upon God Almighty is the guidance to the straight path..."* [16:9]

Works Cited

1. Mohammad bin Abdullah AlNeesaboury, **Al Mustadrak Ala Al Sahihayn**, Dar Al-Kutub Al-Ilmiyah, Beirut, 1990.
2. Abdullah bin Muhammad bin Obeid, **Al Awliya'**, Moassasat AlKutub AlThaqafiya, Beirut, 1992.
3. Suleiman bin Ahmed AlTabarany, **Al Mo'gam Al Kabeer**, Maktabat Aloloum walhikam, Musul, 1983.
4. Abdullah bin Uday Aljarajany, **Al-Kamil Fi Doa'faa Al Rijal**, Dar AlFikr, Beirut, 1988.
5. Ahmed bin Ali AlAsqalany, **Fateh Al Barey**, Dar AlMarifa, Beirut, 1959.
6. Ismail bin Muhammad AlAjlouny, **Kashf al Khafa'**, Moassasat AlRisalah, Beirut, 1984.
7. Ali bin Abi Bakr AlHaithamy, **Majma' al Zawa'id**, Dar AlRayyan LilTurath, Cairo, 1986.
8. Ahmed bin Hanbal Abu Abdullah AlShaybany, **Musnad Ahmad**, Moassasat Qurtoba, (241).
9. Mohammad Ibn Ismail Abu Abdallah Al-Bukhary, **Sahih Al-Bukhari**, Dar Ibn Katheer, Beirut, 1987.
10. Muhammad bin Habban AlTameemy, **Sahih Ibn Habban**, Moassasat AlRisalah, Beirut, 1993.
11. Muslim bin AlHajjaj AlQushairy AlNeesaboury, **Sahih Muslim**, Dar Ihyaa' AlTurath AlAraby, Beirut, (261).
12. Ahmed bin Shuaib AlNasaa'i, **Sunan Al-Nasaa'I**, Maktabat AlMatbouaat AlIslamiya, Halab, 1986.

13. Muhammad bin Yazid AlQazweeny, **Sunan Ibn Majah**, Dar AlFikr, Beirut, (273).
14. Muhammad bin Eisa Abu Eisa AlTirmithi, **Sunan Tirmithi**, Dar Ihyaa' AlTurath AlAraby, Beirut, (279).
15. Ahmed bin Ali bin Hajar AlAsqalany, **Tahzeeb Al Tahzeeb**, Dar AlFikr, Beirut, 1984.

CPSIA information can be obtained at www.ICGtesting.com
Printed in the USA
LVOW10s1835091013

356190LV00007B/460/P